LANDOWNERSHIP in BIRSE

1800 — 1980

The ownership of the 31,000 acres in Birse became steadily more concentrated during the eighteenth century. By 1800 there were only five landowners in the parish: Birse, Finzean, Ballogie and Midstrath estates and the Kirk Session Quarter of Kinminity. A hundred years before there had been fifteen landowners.

The last estate to disappear in the eighteenth century was Balfour. It was sold to the Earl of Aboyne, the owner of Birse estate , by the executors of Alexander Farquharson, the last laird who had died in 1791. His eldest son, Francis Farquharson, was known as the 'Buck of Birse' and it appears that it was his notoriously expensive habits which persuaded the executors to sell.

The exception amongst the five properties in Birse at 1800 was the small Kirk Session Quarter. This had come into the possession of the Kirk Session around 1680 as the result of an unpaid debt dating from 1646. In 1800 it was still run-rigged and these rigs were mixed in with those of the rest of Kinminity, with which the Kirk's Quarter also shared an area of undivided hill ground. The rest of Kinminity had been acquired by the Earl of Aboyne in the 1790s and, on the 24th October 1800, he wrote to the Kirk Session offering to buy their Quarter. He pointed out that if they did not sell he would be obliged to take them to the Court of Session for a division of the run-rig and common lands of Kinminity into consolidated holdings. He did say that he was not trying to use this second very expensive possibility as a "stimulative" towards the first, but stressed that, as the situation was, neither of them could get the best use of their land.

The Kirk Session did not know if they even had the authority to sell their land and so the same week they wrote to both their local Presbytery and to the Procurators of the Church in Edinburgh. Both had replied by December and agreed that it might be wise to sell for the benefit of the poor in the parish. They also said that there was no doubt about the Session's power to sell, but did suggest that a detailed record should be kept so that any later challenge that might arise could be met. In March 1801, the Kirk Session pinned a notice about the Earl's proposals to the Church door so that "no-one concerned might ever pretend ignorance". In April they appointed the surveyor Colin Innes to provide a report on the proposed sale together with a map and suggested value for the Kirk's Quarter. During October Colin Innes came to survey Kinminity and was shown round the lands by the Minister and sitting tenants. In February 1802 he submitted his report. He concluded that in their present condition the lands of the Kirk Quarter would let at about £16 for a nineteen year lease, but that they possessed....

> "a kind of dormant quality.... which although of no value to
> itself adds considerably to the value of Kinminity when the
> whole belongs to one proprietor. Besides the additional value
> which the corn lands will acquire by being possessed so as to

enable the proprietor to divide them in the most eligible mode
for their improvement by trenching, ploughing up baulks (-the
uncultivated strips between the rigs-), corners and large tracts
of the present pasture and uncultivated ground, which, after the
expiry of a lease of the above duration, the value of Kinminity
will be so much increased that at present we can only conjecture
what it may then be, and most probably fall far short of it.
"Independent of the great advantage to be acquired by the
improvement of the arable parts... there is the extensive tract
of hill and muir grounds he acquires for planting, with very
little expense for enclosing or even planting because a very
considerable portion of the marches are already enclosed by
Ballogie and Balfour."

Colin Innes advised that it would be to the mutual advantage of the Kirk Session
and the Earl of Aboyne if the Kirk's Quarter was sold because it could not be
turned to near the same account except by the sale to the proprietor of the
adjoining lands and because it would be equally to his advantage to buy it at
a higher price than it would be worth to any other person. He therefore recommended that "the price ought not to be under what may be considered a high one
at present". He did however point out that, even if the Kirk obtained a very
high price, there was the danger that in....

"perhaps half a century hence, when the face of these fields
is quite altered, and much increased in size, the muir covered
with large thriving woods which will add much pasture, shelter
and warmth to them, and of course to their value, some wise
heads of those days will find out that the Kirk Quarter was
thrown away without ever considering that none of these fields
could have been brought to their then value if the sale under
consideration had not taken place. Who can, twenty years after
this, describe or judge of the present real value of the Kirk
Quarter, when all the cairns and large stones are removed and
built into dykes, all the baulks improved along with large
pieces of the pasture ground into corn lands, the whole surface
laid out in a regular improved state. It is not too much to
say that the very people who shall execute these operations
will not be able to describe them so as to make a stranger to
judge of the subject we are now valuing. If this shall be the
case twenty years hence, how much more shall it be fifty years
afterwards."

A meeting of the Kirk Session, of which the Earl was a member, was called on
the 30th September 1802 to consider Colin Innes' report...

"The meeting then fixed upon a price under which they were
not to sell their property - namely £500 - the Earl of Aboyne
having previously retired from the meeting. Upon the Earl's
return to the meeting he offered the very sum which the
meeting had fixed upon for its value, upon which they
unanimously agreed to accept the same, being upwards of
thirty five years purchase of the lands at Mr. Innes'
valuation, after deducting the public burdens, being
equal to the rate or price at which land sells in this
country at the present time."

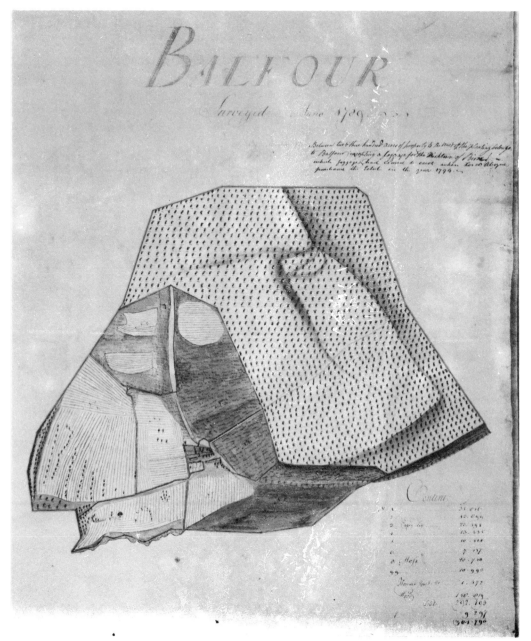

Fig.A.   A map of Balfour estate when it was surveyed in 1789.
The area shown is 301 acres and excludes 200-300 acres to
the west of the plantation. The Kirktown of Birse had foggage
over that extra area, but the foggage ceased to exist when
the Earl of Aboyne bought Balfour in 1794.

Fig.B.   Balfour in 1840 showing its full extent of over 600 acres.
The 94 acres of arable are held by a single tenant.

Fig.C.   Kinminity in 1840, consisting of over 600 acres. The arable
area of just over 100 acres is shared between eight tenants,
whose fields are intermixed.

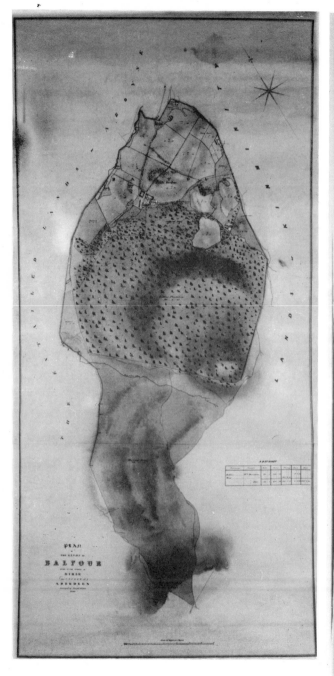

Fig.B

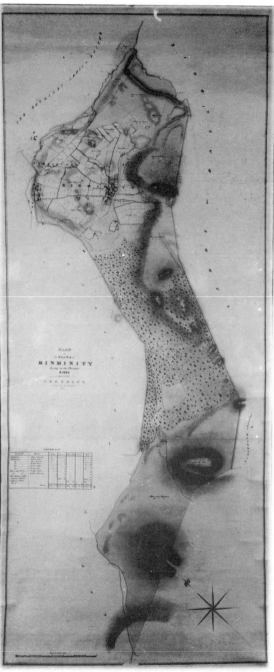

Fig.C

It was then agreed that "the price is to remain in the hands of his Lordship" and that he would pay five percent interest,upon it as a loan, even though the Minister had to use his own money to pay Colin Innes' bill of £10.17.6 and wait to be repaid when the Earl made his first interest payment.

The sale does not seem to have been popular locally and Colin Innes' prediction of peoples' attitude in "perhaps half a century hence" was also borne out. Robert Dinnie wrote of the Kirk's Quarter in 1864 "this small property was sold... it is said to the no small astonishment and displeasure of the majority of the parishioners - having been done without their consent either sought or obtained. But of course the Session could have no idea that land would have risen so much in value as it has done since that time".

Long before Dinnie wrote that, however, the Earl of Aboyne had already sold the land. In 1840, the Earl, by then also the eighth Marquis of Huntly, went bankrupt and both Kinminity and Balfour were sold to Francis Cochran (1809-70), an advocate in Aberdeen. He was a kinsman of the Marquis through his mother, but also, he was married to Elizabeth, the great grand-daughter of Alexander Farquharson whose executors had sold Balfour to the Marquis. This estate of Balfour and Kinminity has remained with the Cochrans ever since, though since the Second World War half of it has been feued to the Forestry Commission so that it now only extends to 450 acres. The present laird is the fifth generation.

Alexander Farquharson of Balfour, whose eldest son was the 'Buck of Birse', had another son, William, and he succeeded to Finzean estate where the mainline had died out with the death of Francis Farquharson. The Farquharsons still own Finzean estate, although the succession has been erratic at times, for example, in the 1930s it passed to a second cousin and then to his nephew. The present laird is the thirteenth Farquharson of Finzean. The changes in the extent of the estate within Birse since the eighteenth century have been small. Auchabrack was sold to Ballogie in the 1930s and the Shannel (467 acres) to Ian Alcock in 1973/4; in the 1950s Easter Clune wood was feued to the Forestry Commission. The present extent of the estate is about 7,900 acres.

The history of Ballogie estate has also involved Farquharsons. In 1789 it was bought by Charles Innes, the second son of James Innes and Catherine Gordon of Balnacraig. He appears to have been a problem child as he was twice sent off to the Scots College at Douai in France. The first time he ran away and then the second time he was sent home. However, while he may not have been suited for priesthood, he was a successful businessman. He went to St. Petersburg. Russia, and amassed a considerable fortune. In 1787 he returned and secured Balnacraig by paying off the family's debts and in 1789 he purchased the adjacent estate of Ballogie, after the sudden death of its owner Mr. Forbes.

Charles Innes died in 1803 and was succeeded by his elder brother Lewis, who died in 1815. Ballogie and Balnacraig then passed to their nearest of kin, a cousin, Lewis Farquharson, a brother of James Farquharson, laird of Balmoral and Inverey. He had been a merchant in Canada, but he returned home to settle at Ballogie and assume the name and arms of the Innes of Balnacraig. His wife was the daughter of an Irishman, Mackveagh. who had a large scale linen manufacturing business at Huntly. Lewis (Farquharson) Innes died in 1830, aged 67. He was succeeded by his only son, Lewis, who died suddenly in 1844 at the age of 34. The estate then fell to his sisters, three Miss Farquharsons living at Ballogie and a Mrs. Lynch in London. In 1852 they sold Ballogie and Balnacrag to James Dyce Nicol.

The neighbouring estate of Midstrath, which had included Auchaballa and Muirley from Balfour since 1740, had been bought by James Gerard in the mid eighteenth century. He was succeeded by his brother and then, successively, by his three grandsons, the eldest of whom died at Waterloo while proprietor. They were succeeded by their cousin, James Gerard, who sold the estate to James Dyce Nicol in 1862. The estates of Ballogie, Balnacraig and Midstrath are still owned by the Nicols and amount to about 6,000 acres.

The other estate in the parish, Birse estate, which had been bought by the first Earl of Aboyne in 1666, was sold by the trustees of his descendant, the seventh Earl of Aboyne and tenth Marquis of Huntly, in 1897. It was bought by an American Joseph Robert Heaven and his Spanish wife, who lived at 24 Grosvenor Square in the City of Westminster, for £40,000. They also acquired with the lands in Birse, several houses around the end of the suspension bridge in Aboyne, including the Huntly Lodge which they renamed 'Forest of Birse Lodge'. They had four sons, the eldest of whom, Captain Robert Heaven, died before his parents. The second son, Joseph Heaven, became Count Ramirez de Orellano by succession through his mother.

In 1911, after Joseph Robert Heaven's death, his three surviving sons sold his lands in Birse to Baron Cowdray of Midhurst, Sussex, for £52,000. At that time, Baron Cowdray was just about to go to Mexico and 'might not return for sometime', so he granted power of attorney to a Writer of the Signet in Edinburgh and had the estate conveyed to his wife Annie, Baroness Cowdray. The estate still remains with the Cowdrays, a small part of the hundred square miles they own in Aberdeenshire alone. In 1978, the current Viscount Cowdray sold the Birse estate to his son, the Hon. Charles Pearson.

The Mortification of Dr. Gilbert Ramsay ──

From time to time Birse has benefitted from donations by individuals who have left the parish in their youth and achieved success overseas. One of the earliest and most generous of these benefactors was Dr. Gilbert Ramsay.

He graduated from Aberdeen University in the 1670s and went on to become Rector of Christ's Church in Barbados, where he also owned a plantation. From 1713 onwards he donated money to Aberdeen University and to Birse, the final sum and arrangements being given in his will of 1728, after he had retired to Bath a wealthy man.

In his grants Gilbert Ramsay describes Birse as the place of his 'nativity', but the exact nature of his family connection to the parish is not clear. He was, however, a member of the landowning class and so related to many of the important families in the North-east. He was a descendant of Sir Gilbert Ramsay of Balmain, cousin to the Marquis of Montrose. It was Sir Gilbert's daughter who was reputed to have tried to help Montrose escape in 1650. Dr. Gilbert's closest apparent relations in Birse were the Ochterlonies of Tillyfruskie, who were cousins by marriage through the Buchans of Auchmacoy.

The patronage of Dr. Gilbert Ramsay's bequests was left in 1728 to the Ramsays of Balmain, the then laird, Sir Alexander, being a first cousin. It was a condition of all Gilbert Ramsay's bursaries at the University that they should first be given to a Ramsay or, failing that, to any inhabitant of the parish of Birse: a stipulation that benefitted at least three members of the unrelated family of Ramsays at Birsemore.

Gilbert Ramsay's will left £4,800, which was to be used to purchase land on the edge of New Aberdeen. The yearly rent from this was then to be employed to the benefit of Marischal College and Birse. At the University this was to provide the salary to found a Chair of Hebrew and Oriental Languages, to provide bursaries for four students of Divinity and to supplement his 1714 grant of four bursaries in Greek and Philosophy. These arrangements were not without their problems.

In 1729, Sir Alexander Ramsay won a legal dispute over who should have the power of selection of the Professor and Bursars. In 1736 he won another lawsuit, after the Professor of Divinity had turned away three students Sir Alexander had put forward, because they had not brought certificates of moral character and education from their Presbytery. It was also noted at the time that, while Gilbert Ramsay had been one of the University's most generous benefactors, it had been a mistake to make the criteria "interest" (i.e. Ramsay/Birse) alone and not the ability or poverty of the students. This had been abused by students who attended a course of Divinity just to draw the bursary money, while really studying for another subject.

Gilbert Ramsay's first gift to Birse was made in the mid 1720s when he supplied funds through the University for a five arch stone bridge to be built across the Feugh at Whitestones. It was subsequently swept away seventy years later in the flood of 1799. He also wrote to the Birse Kirk Session at that time to enquire about the expense of founding and endowing an hospital in the parish to support a number of aged people. However, the Session, from 'motives of delicacy', declined to do so and events were overtaken by Dr. Ramsay's will which established his Mortification in 1732.

The will provided that the income from £500 of the £4,800 should be used for the support of the poor in the parish. Another £500 was to provide the salary for the appointment of a 'pious, prudent and experienced' schoolmaster in Birse. The first year's income was, however, to be used to build a school in the most convenient place - which the Session decided was Bankhead. Both these gifts benefitted the inhabitants of Birse for nearly two centuries.

Gilbert Ramsay's generous will also included several other items not related to the University or Birse. For example, £500 was left to his parish in Barbados for the education and training of apprentices in useful trades. There was £25 for each of his Executors in Barbados 'so each could all have a suit of mourning'. There was another £25 to each of his two godsons and goddaughters so they could each buy a young negro woman slave.

Gilbert Ramsay also stipulated in his will that all his slaves, except his negro manservant Robert, whom he had brought with him to Bath, should be sold at a cheaper rate than normal to those who would look after them well. On Dr. Ramsay's death the slave Robert was to receive his freedom, a paid passage back to Barbados and £5 to set him up. This was a hundred and five years before slavery was abolished.

The Nicols

The name Nicol derives from the clan Macnacail or MacNical, which traditionally held land in the extreme north-west of Scotland. The cohesion of this clan and their lands in Durness, Assynt and Edderachylis was lost when the daughter of the last chief married a son of the chief of the clan Macloed. There were also frequent and severe fights with the MacIntoshes and around 1600 many Nicols came south from Sutherland.

Many of these Nicols settled in Aberdeenshire and Kincardineshire, although some went as far south as Glasgow. By the end of the 1600s there were half a dozen families of Nicols living in Birse. They were tenants or subtenants at Tilly-garmond, Balfidy, Wester Clune, Muirley and Glencat. The present owners of Ballogie, however, trace their descent at that time to a Nicol who was a tenant farmer at Arbuthnott in Kincardineshire.

Wm. Nicol (1692-1753) was a farmer at Bringieshill. He was survived by three sons. The eldest, Robert (born 1724) was the tenant at Craighill and then Hareden (1760) in the same parish. The youngest, William (1747-1815) died the tenant of Bringieshill, one of his sons becoming the tenant of Mains of Barras, Kineff.

James Nicol (1734-1808), the middle son, was also a tenant of Bringieshill for some years, but later became the Overseer on Arbuthnott Estate. In 1764 he married Elizabeth Rankine (1733-1812), the daughter of a tenant farmer at Dunnotar. In 1783 James became tenant of Fawsyde, Kineff, which he farmed until his death. They had four children, the last two of whom were twins Helen and Andrew. Helen (born 1769) married the farmer at Mains of Catterline, Kineff, while Andrew (1769-1837), who married the daughter of an Aberdeen Baillie, stayed in Montrose becoming a Burgess.

William Nicol (1765-1827) and James (1767-1849) were the other two children. James succeeded his father as tenant of Fawsyde, but then moved to Banff to become a Collector of Taxes. He was twice married. In 1789 to the daughter of an Aberdeen builder and then in 1816 to Margaret Stephenson, a relation of a well-known North-east clergyman. He had one son by each marriage. William (1790-1879) was born at Fawsyde and married his first cousin Margaret Dyce Nicol, daughter of his uncle William. He went to India and in 1820 settled in Bombay where he founded the firm of Wm. Nicol & Co. In 1839 he returned to England a rich man and became a Director of several companies, including the London and County Bank. He was M.P. for Dover (1859-65) and a J.P. and Deputy Lord Lieutenant for Kincardineshire, before he died in London at the age of 89. He and his wife left no issue. His half brother, Andrew (1819-89), who had been a merchant in Colombo, Ceylon, and then the owner of several plantations there, died in Elgin.

William Nicol (above) obtained an M.A. and M.D. from Aberdeen. For a short time he was a surgeon in the R.N. but he then settled down in 1792 as a medical practicioner in Stonehaven. He took a keen interest in county affairs and was a Captain in the local militia, as well as a Commissioner of Income and Property Tax. In 1794 he married Margaret Dyce (1772-1841), the only child of James Dyce an Aberdeen merchant and Burgess, who owned Badentoy Estate. They had one son and six daughters. All the daughters married except one. Margaret married her cousin William in Bombay. Christina married a partner in the same firm. Mary's husband became a General, while Jane and Elizabeth married merchants in Glasgow and Liverpool.

James Dyce Nicol (1805-1872), their only son, entered the Bombay firm of Wm. Nicol & Co. when he was sixteen and five years later he became a partner. In 1838 he left Bombay and by 1844 he had retired from the company. The same year he married Catherine Lloyd (1815-1905), the daughter of a Manchester banker. In 1850 he added Ballogie and Balnacraig to the estate of Badentoy which he had inherited from his father. In 1859 he purchased Newtonhill and Gillybrands as well as adding the adjacent property of CairnRobin to Badentoy. In 1863 he added Midstrath to Ballogie and was M.P. for Kincardineshire 1865-72. He and his wife had three sons. The youngest, Lewis (1858-1935), succeeded to the estates of Newtonhill and Gillybrands in 1883. He was married to Agnes, eldest daughter of Sir Sanford Freeling, K.C.M.G., and followed a military career, becoming a Brigadier General. The second son, James (born 1848), was an East Indian Merchant 1871-92 and married Alice Warden, the daughter of a senior member of the Bombay Legislative Council. He succeeded to Badentoy and became a J.P. and Deputy Lord Lieutenant for Kincardineshire.

William Edward Nicol (1846-1914), the eldest son, succeeded to Ballogie and Balnacraig. He became a Lt.Colonel in the London Scottish. He was a Commissioner of Supply for Aberdeenshire and then served several terms on the County Council. He was a J.P. for both Aberdeenshire and Kincardineshire and a Deputy Lord Lt. for the latter. He married Catherine Lewis in 1873. She was the only child of John Wm. Prout. The Prouts had owned land in Gloucestershire since the time of Elizabeth I, and her grandfather was the celebrated Victorian chemist Wm. Prout. She was a cousin and heiress of Joseph Nicoll of Neasden, Middlesex, a Moneyer at the Mint. They had four children and were survived by two daughters and a son. One of these daughters, Dorothy, died a spinster, the other married a Warner.

Randall James Nicol (1882-1941), their son, joined the Scottish Horse in 1904 and served in the Argyll and Sutherland Highlanders with distinction during the First World War. He was awarded an O.B.E. on demobilisation. He served on the Deeside District Council and, after 1929, on the Deeside District Committee. He was a J.P. and Deputy Lord Lieutenant for Kincardineshire, Chairman of the Income Tax Commission for Aberdeenshire and at one time a Director of Aberdeen Newspapers Ltd. He was never married and on his death, the estate passed to his nephew, John Warner (born 1912), who assumed the name of Nicol on his succession and is the present Laird of Ballogie.

Colonel John Nicol, D.S., D.L., was the second son of the marriage between Marjory Nicol, Randall Nicol's other sister, and Sir George Redston Warner, K.C.V.O., C.M.G., (1879-1978). Sir George was the son of Sir Joseph Warner (1836-1897), a barrister who became Counsel to the Chairman of Committees at the House of Lords. Sir George had a distinguished career in the Foreign Service as did his eldest son, Colonel Nicol's elder brother, Sir Edward Redston Warner, K.C.M.G., C.M.G., (born 1911), who was British Ambassador to Tunisia 1968-70.

King Dardanus

and his Stone

Near the highest point of the road from Marywell to Feughside, stands the stone of King Dardanus. It was first uncovered and set up on its present site towards the close of the eighteenth century. About fifty years later, it was broken in two by workmen, during road improvements. The then laird of Finzean, Archibald Farquharson, ordered that the pieces be restored and the stone replaced in its original position. This was done: the stone was clamped together with iron bars, and thus it remains to this day, defiant, rugged, weatherbeaten, facing onto the more polished edifice of the parish War Memorial.

The Dardanus Stone is said by tradition to mark the place where a tyrant of that name was defeated in battle and executed by his own subjects. His story is contained in the voluminous pages of Hector Boece's History of the Scots, first published in 1527. This is a narrative of the supposed deeds of Scottish monarchs stretching from pre-Roman times to the death of the first King James in 1437.

Dardanus (as he was called in Boece's original classical Latin) was, we are told, not of direct royal line, but had been chosen to rule the Scots while the three young princes of the blood were being educated on the Isle of Man. He was regarded as a man of honour and was famous for his vast bulk:

> 'Ane man he wes of greit nobillitie,
> And in his corss of rycht greit quantitie;
> Bayth large and lang, rycht greit and gross withall
> Quhairfoir to name Grand Dardane tha him call.'

> Scots metric translation of Boece by Hellenden,
> et seq.

For two years, Dardanus ruled well, being particularly gracious to those of noble blood. In the third year of his reign, however, he "changit intill ane uther man", and became "ane cruell king". This abrupt volte-face was the work of his evil favourite, Conan. Thereafter, Dardanus indulged himself in a life of vicious high living, enriching evil men, and arranging the murder of "ane greit man of gude" left over from the previous reign.

> "He grew so wickit and so full of will,
> So odious till all man and so ill,
> That everie man him haittit to the deid,
> And as thair fa had him at als greit feid".

His downfall soon followed. Dardanus sent one of his henchmen to the Isle of Man to assassinate the royal princes, but the henchman was arrested at the point of plunging a dagger into the back of one of them, and confessed to his captors that King Dardanus was behind the deed.

The Lords of Scotland plotted against the tyrannical king and led an army to topple him from the throne. On the battlefield, Dardanus' former associates ran away and the evil Conan was taken and hanged like a thief. In despair, Dardanus drew a knife to kill himself. But two of his former servants prevented him, and brought him, bound hand and foot, to the feet of the royal princes. He was shown no mercy: off went his head, at the stroke of "ane braid ax". It was stuck on a spear, and carried about the host by "ane carle that stalwart wes and stout". His body was cast into a deep well, and "thus he endit for his wickit deid". He perished in the fourth year of his reign in 75AD. (not 81AD as some guidebooks state).

So much for the career of wicked King Dardanus. It would be quite fruitless to speculate whether any of this account is true. Boece's narrative is presented to us as history, but he was in fact writing myth and legend. The Dardanus story closely resembles that of Macbeth, which is less remarkable than might otherwise appear, since an English translation of Boece was Shakespeare's main source for his play. Boece had a rather limited imagination and, like a modern hack novelist, tended to use the same story over and over again. Even in his own age, many learned contemporaries regarded his 'history' as wholly bogus.

Boece, however, had a wholly serious purpose. His History, which took ten years to write, was based on the Roman History of Livy and was couched in a similar melodramatic style. It was intended to dignify the Scottish monarchy, by displaying an ancestral antiquity comparable to France and the Holy Roman Empire and - incidentally - far outstripping that of the English throne. Boece's own king, James V, was delighted with the work and rewarded him with a pension.

However did this obscure, mythical king become associated with the stone by the Marywell road? The attribution of prominent stones to the death place of ancient warriors and kings is in itself not unusual. In neighbouring parishes to Birse, Macbeth's Stone, Lulach's Stone and Earl Davy's Stone all commemmorate, with varying degrees of probability, the spot where these persons met their death wounds. Quite often, such stones are accompanied by cairns which romantic historians like to interpret as evidence of an ancient battle. Now there is nothing in Boece's narrative to link the death of Dardanus with any particular area. Indeed, if anything, Boece contradicts the Birse tradition that Dardanus was buried beneath the stone, since he states that his body was denied burial because of the king's wicked deeds, and cast into a well. However there are, or used to be, two large cairns and a stone circle on the hillside near the site of Dardanus' Stone which were thought to be associated with the king's death. Moreover, the name of Corsedardar Hill is suggestive, and herein may lie the clue to the local tradition.

An obvious guess is that Corsedardar Hill was named after Boece's mythical king. We do not know how old the name 'Corsedardar' is but it could, and probably does, predate the time of Boece. The Marywell-Feughside corse or hill crossing is an ancient one. Tillyfruskie, "the knoll of the crossing" in Finzean, is mentioned in a charter of 1170. The area, possibly even the stone itself, might even then have been associated with a real or imaginary personage called "Dardar". The Den of Dardar near Aberdour evidently commemmorates the same character; the reader may know of other examples. It may very well be that Boece borrowed the name, and did not supply the tradition at all.

Hector Boece sometimes used details of local geography to add verisimilitude to his stories. He presided over the university at Aberdeen, where most of his history was written, and appears to have travelled about the north-east and known its traditions. Perhaps one day, as he was wracking his brains to conjure up yet more bogus names to fill in the missing centuries, he remembered Corse Dardar. The very thing! By nightfall his inkwell was dry, and the stock story of a big, bad king called Dardanus had been born.

Once all the mythical accretions of Boece and his successors have been sloughed away, there remains a possibility that once, long ago, there lived an important person called Dardar who dwelt in Birse and whose grave was marked by a large stone. But if that is so, we know nothing whatever about him.

JOHN GORDON OF GLENCAT

John Gordon was born in 1702, the second son of the laird of Glencat. His father, also named John, had been a merchant in rented property at Mill of Kincardine until 1699 when he managed to buy Glencat. It was a small estate of less than half a dozen tenant families, but the Aberdeenshire Poll Book shows that it was nevertheless considered a Gentleman's residence.

John Gordon's parents both died when he was very young - his father when he was only two and his mother, Jean Gordon, before he was eight. John was then left under the guardianship of his elder brother who sent him off to school in Kincardine O'Neil.

John's family, in the Gordon tradition, were all devout Roman Catholics. Despite this, or possibly because of it, he grew up with an intense dislike of the ritual and superstition of the papist religion, and after three years at school he ran away to Aberdeen to escape his religious education. He was about eleven at the time. There he stayed with the family of a young friend he had made in Kincardine O'Neil, James Strachan. James' father, Thomas Strachan, was an alderman in the Town but kept some land at the Kirktown of Kincardine which was owned by a close relation, John Strachan.

The Strachans were ardent and pious Protestants and John happily joined in with the family worship at his new home. However, John's kinsmen were keeping a close eye on his movements. They had already made one or two unsuccessful attempts at kidnapping him when one day, as John was going out to the fields, he was abducted by a group of four horsemen led by his uncle, Alexander Gordon of Barrack, New Deer.

At New Deer John's religious education was restarted by his relations who tended to excuse his earlier behaviour as merely youthful folly. John had little choice but to obey yet secretly he looked for ways of escaping. He managed to get in contact with the local Protestant Minister, John Webster, and with his help attempted to return to Aberdeen.

However, John was recaptured by his relations after a cross country chase. This time many of them did not feel so forgiving. They went so far as to accuse him of being a heretic and demanded that he serve public penance. In the end, however, out of consideration for his uncle's standing, it was decided that he would instead have to perform half a dozen 'Pater Nosters' and 'Ave Maria's' each day for two months.

John was given little opportunity to escape this time. By the time he was thirteen he adopted a new strategy: he asked to be allowed to go to sea. This seemed to meet with the general approval of his family and, to his surprise, his uncle also agreed: on one condition. On taking leave of his relations, John must include a visit to his first cousin Robert Gordon, Chaplain to the Duke of Gordon. The reason for this condition was soon made apparent. When John reached his cousin's house he discovered that the Chaplain had organised some people to escort him north to a papist school at Strathdown in the Highlands.

For a year, John sojourned in unwilling captivity at Strathdown. Then came unexpected good news. He was told he was leaving to join a ship at Aberdeen on which a passage had been arranged for him. He was duly taken to the ship but, when he went on board, he discovered to his horror that there were three other young Scottish gentlemen there bound over to deliver John to the Scottish Catholic College in Paris.

John Gordon was at the Paris College for thirteen years. When his time came to take the Order of Priesthood, his examination was conducted by the Archbishop of Notre Dame and attended by all the Catholic hierarchy. The Archbishop asked John, at the conclusion of the interview, whether he received the Catholic Constitution and looked upon it as a Rule of Faith. Emboldened by his long suffering, John answered by denying Catholicism. There was an immediate uproar. Cries of heretic broke out from the throng of witnesses. In the confusion John somehow managed to slip away. He went into hiding for some days and then escaped towards the Channel, arriving in England in April 1731, aged 29.

He made his way north to Edinburgh and, by June of that year, had secured a testimonial from the Presbytery acknowledging that he had renounced popery and embraced the Protestant religion. The same week he also took the precaution of obtaining a letter of protection from the Lord Chief Justice, Adam Cockburn of Ormiston.

The letter states that "John Gordon is returning to Aberdeen about his lawful affairs but being apprehensive that he may be insulted by some persons on account of his renouncing the papish religion" it goes on to command "all Sheriffs of Shires, Stewarts of Stewartries, Bailies of Baillaries and Royalties, and their respective deputies, Justices of His Majesties Peace and Magistrates of Burghs not only to suffer Mr. John Gordon to pass about his lawful business but also to aid and assist him".

What lawful affairs John Gordon had in mind are unknown, but three years later he had a Memoir published in London "wherein the absurdities and delusions of papery are laid open... and the Infallibility of the Romish Church is confuted.. with also an appendix containing some short but full Answers to any Question that can be proposed by a papist". The last we hear of John Gordon of Glencat is the prefixed publisher's note which says the author is now in London ready to vindicate what he has written.

Habitat: The Shooting Green ───────────

The Shooting Greens is a name given to the rough ground between the Potarch-Whitestones road and the Dee, and bounded on the west and east by the Grinnoch and Kettock burns. Opinions differ on how its name was acquired. Some say that archer's butts were set up here on the orders of King James IV in the days preceding Flodden Field. Others that it was simply a place where parishioners went to shoot a hare or partridge for the pot. The Reverend Joseph Smith, who wrote the Old Statistical Account of Birse (1791), refers to the Shooting Greens as if it were a familiar name to his contemporaries. The older and more strictly correct name for the area is Slewdrum, or 'Glensleudrum'. Slewdrum probably derives from sliabh druim, meaning 'moor ridge', and must date back to Gaelic-speaking days, which in Birse would have been the fifteenth century or earlier. The unorthodox spelling of 'Sleudrum' somehow led to its transcription as 'Lendrum', under which name it appears in a number of title deeds.

The Potarch-Whitestones road which passes by the Shooting Greens, giving access from Deeside to the Cairn o' Mounth, was an important drove road at least as long ago as the seventeenth century and probably before. There is an early record of a Birse fair in 1662, and a regular traffic of cattle, sheep, horses and cloth-bearing wagons must have forded the Dee at Inchbare (now Potarch) and flowed over the Shooting Greens on their way south to the trysts at Crieff and Falkirk. Large scale cattle droving took place from the middle years of the eighteenth century. The animals using this route would usually have originated either locally or in Donside and Strathbogie, although early snowfalls might have forced drovers from further north and west to use the Cairn o' Mounth. Sheep began to increase at the expense of cattle in the first half of the nineteenth century, and continued to be driven along the old routes until the growth of the railway network brought about an abrupt decline in their use. The Shooting Greens road must have been at its busiest in the years after 1814, when the parish market stance was moved from Marywell to Potarch. The reason for this was, of course, the long-delayed construction of Potarch bridge over the Dee which vastly improved communications between the north Deeside turnpike and the parish of Birse.

The Shooting Greens has always been a Crown common, which was different from the majority of pieces of common ground, known as commonties, which existed in Scotland before the nineteenth century. On commonties it was only a parish's heritors, and through them their tenants, who had common rights such as grazing, fuel and divot. On the Shooting Greens anyone, over and above the rights of the people in Strachan and Birse, could use it as a grazing stance. It must have been heavily used when the Cairn o' Mounth was an active drove route, but it was still being used by some of Deeside's flockmasters into this century. They used it as an overnight stop when driving sheep away from the Aboyne Marts or else when taking sheep to winter grazings to the east and south of Birse. One of them, Dod Grant, who used the Shooting Greens until the 1950s, spent much of the winter between September and May there with his flock of four or five hundred ewes.

The Shooting Green survived as a relic common long after other areas because it was a Crown Common. The commonties could be cheaply and quickly divided amongst neighbouring landowners following a 1695 Act of the Scottish Parliament, so that the Lord Advocate could report in 1828 that "There is very little property in Scotland that is now common". It was not, however, until 1829 that any legislation was created for the division of Crown commons and, because of this late date and the scarcity of Crown commons, one or two survived into this century, when their administration was taken over by the Crown Commissioners.

The Forestry Commission bought Blackhall estate in the 1930s and was subsequently granted the pasturage and servitude of the adjoining Shooting Greens by the Commissioner of Crown Lands. However, the two other neighbouring estates, Ballogie and Finzean, retained and upheld their rights under existing utilisation. These included grazings and fishing (both estates), the building of "shiels" (Finzean) or "cottages" (Ballogie), and rights to fuel, feal, divot, cutting timber and "fowling" (Ballogie). In addition, Ballogie estate owned the Solum or land surface of the "Moss of Strathseven". This meant that the Forestry Commission did not plant their first tree until 1960, when the estates agreed to surrender their rights, except for the fishings and the grazings on two specified areas.

Little is known about the early vegetation of the Shooting Greens. When the Reverend Joseph Smith (1791) described those upland areas of the parish where "our frugal swains do literally feed their flocks", he added that "the hills produce a variety of herbs" but that their "names and virtues we cannot pretend to specify". Judging from old maps however, the Shooting Greens cannot have supported many trees for at least three or four centuries, apart from some patches of scrub and a narrow strip of wood along the banks of the Dee, which remains in a natural condition to this day.

The Forestry Commission's plantings of 1960/61 meant that Slewdrum was once again a forest in fact as well as name. The crop trees were predominantly Scots Pine together with stands of foreign trees like Sitka and Norway Spruce, Douglas and Grand Fir, Lodgepole Pine and Larch. A band of larch was planted to 'soften' the visual impact of the uncompromisingly straight western margin where, significantly in terms of the natural history interest, a belt along the Dee access track and roadside was left unplanted. This surviving area of 'wild ground' included the western slopes of Little Ord, between Coulnacraig and the Dee, and the wet meadow in the kink of the road, the last fragment of the 'Moss of Strathseven'. The Little Ord slopes consisted of small copses of birch, willow, rowan and alder, much of which had regenerated since the decline in grazing, together with a mosaic of wet grasslands and heaths.

Undoubtedly the most intriguing wild flower of the Shooting Greens is the Whorled Caraway, Carum verticillatum. Although it bears rather ordinary umbelliferous flowers, its capillary leaves with their whorls of wiry segments are quite unmistakable. The Caraway was not known to nineteenth century local botanists and appears not to have been discovered here until the 1950s, when it was found almost simultaneously by Professor V.C. Wynne-Edwards and Mrs. Alice Sommerville.

The significance of the discovery lies in the fact that the Shooting Greens remains the Caraway's one and only locality in eastern Scotland, although it is frequent, very locally, on some of the hill pastures of the west coast. The Shooting Greens site is so far removed from the plant's normal natural range in Britain that it is reasonable to suppose that it must have been introduced from elsewhere. In the light of the history of the Shooting Greens, it appears likely that the Caraway was brought in as seeds in the wool or droppings of sheep, probably during the nineteenth century, when the Greens were a foraging stance for animals bound on the long road over the Mounth to the trysts. Admittedly, west coast sheep were not taken to the markets by this route very often, but one instance could have been enough: the wet grassy hillsides of the Shooting Greens closely resemble the Caraway's natural pastures in the far west.

The Whorled Caraway now thrives in the wet meadows by the Forestry Commission firepond, and on the grassy slopes of Little Ord, although it is apparently confined to the northern side of the road. The cessation of livestock grazing after the war probably favoured the spread of the plant, by allowing it to ripen and disperse its seeds. The Forestry Commission plantings of 1960/61 diminished the amount of habitat available to it, but there must nevertheless be tens of thousands of Caraway plants at the Shooting Greens.

A second notable aspect of the natural history of the Shooting Greens is its unusually large populations of wild orchids. There are probably two reasons for this. One is the unusual quantity of limestone in this area; indeed, as Joseph Smith points out, Birse is 'abounding with limestone', with quarries at Midstrath, Ballogie and one near the Shooting Greens itself. The percolation of lime-rich water down the open slopes towards the Burn of Grinnoch is favourable to calci-colous or 'lime-loving' plants, which include many of our orchids. The other reason may be an abundance of mycorhizal fungus in the soil, which orchids require for the germination of their dust-like seeds. In consequence, the Shoot-ing Greens can boast at least eight species, among them the Early Purple, Lesser Butterfly, Heath Spotted and Northern Marsh Orchids. The most recent discovery was made during a Scottish Wildlife Trust visit to the site in June 1982, when a colony of Bird's Nest Orchids, of which there is only one other known site in Aberdeenshire, was found in the shade of a patch of birch scrub.

Orchids are not the only lime-loving plants to be found on the Shooting Greens. Patches of tall herb vegetation by the Burn of Grinnoch contain the butter-yellow balls of Globeflower, while the banks of the Dee have, in places, a relatively rich flora: a stretch near Potarch contains one hundred and fifty species of wild flowers and ferns. For one lime-loving mountain plant, the Yellow Mountain Saxifrage, the Shooting Greens was the most eastern locality in the country. Unfortunately it grew close to the area where the Forestry Commission chose to place their car park and picnic site and a recent search failed to find the saxifrage. The Forestry Commission made further plantings on the Shooting Greens in 1982, so that now only small fragments remain unplanted. Fortunately the Caraway and Bird's Nest Orchid sites, together with much of the existing birch and willow scrub, were left intact. The Commission also planted some broadleaves, such as rowan, gean and alder, for amenity. However, the greenery of the Shooting Greens is now provided not by stretches of open grass but by the shades of the tight packed crop trees, and most of its natural character has been lost. Some of its wild flora and fauna remain in limited areas, but relics of its past use by people, such as the Soldiers Well and woodcutters' turf bothies, have been buried beneath the uniform blanket of conifers.

THE MEIKLE DROUTH OF 1826

In 1825 the population of Birse was at its highest ever level with nearly 1600 people living in the parish. Then, in 1826, an unprecedented drought burnt up the crops. During the winter of that year and through to the summer of 1827, there was a great scarcity of all provisions. Not for over a hundred years had there been such famine. What little oats there were from the harvest were eaten by the farmers and their families to keep themselves alive, none could even be saved for the next year's seed.

A great proportion of the parish's horses and black cattle died. Furze (gorse) and heath tops were cut to keep some alive, but many were so weak they died when they were taken out to labour the ground for the next season's crop. Others that lasted into the spring of 1827 died of inflammation and related causes when they again began to find fresh growth. Some farmers went to the length of importing hay from Holland, but only the wealthiest could afford the 2/3 per stone.

By April 1827, the Minister noted "In a word, the distress can scarcely be described". Yet despite this, the Kirk Session was frustrated in its ambition to help because the money it was owed by the parish's two major landowners had not been paid. The Earl of Aboyne still had the £500 with which he had bought the Kirk Quarter of Kinminity and he had not paid the instalment of interest then due on it. The Kirk Session also wanted £20 of the capital sum repaid to assist in their urgent relief work, but could not obtain this as the Earl was living in London.

Finzean Estate owed £15 as the accumulated interest from a sum of £20 Mortified by the late Robert Farquharson. The annual interest was so small that it had only ever been taken up in a year of scarcity. Now nine years interest were due but attempts to collect it were unsuccessful. Archibald Farquharson had had to put the estate in Trust and the Edinburgh accountant, Claude Russell Esq., who collected the half term rents, "advanced several excuses, so that payment was not obtained".

The only meal in the parish was being brought in from Stonehaven and Aberdeen by those who could afford it. The Minister had to advance £20 of his own money to help those on the Poor Roll. The most active relief however, was being undertaken by the people themselves through the Wright Friendly Society of Birse. They were very active in laying out funds to purchase and bring into the parish meal, or oats to be ground into meal, for their members and any others in distress.

The situation steadily improved through the summer of 1827 and a good hairst was gathered that autumn. However, just two years after the Meikle Drouth, due to the unprecedented floods of the Muckle Spate, hardship was back again.

THE MARKET ——————
————— AT MARYWELL

Until the early nineteenth century Marywell was in many ways the focus of the parish. It was a hamlet with a score of houses inhabited by farmers, merchants, innkeepers, blacksmiths, carpenters, weavers, tailors, excise officers, carriers and others. The three Birse markets also used to be held there in May, October and November. One was the Foot Market held near the site of the present dwelling house and another was the Cattle Market at a spot now covered with trees a short distance to the east.

The markets continued at Marywell until 1814 when they were removed to Potarch after the bridge was built. By the mid nineteenth century the old houses that had clustered around the commutation road at Marywell had entirely disappeared and been replaced by just a few new ones. In 1860 the Inn which had been kept at Marywell since time immemorial had its license withdrawn. A few years later Robert Dinnie wrote a poem recalling a childhood visit to 'The Market at Marywell'....

MARYWELL MARKET.

Whan I was a youngster o' five or sax years,
Wi' a kiltie as short as the Heilander wears;
My spawls they were naked as whan I was born,
Weel bronzed wi' the sun an' sometimes something torn.
A touzie white pow like the snaw on Bena'nn,
The hair whiddin' roun' wi' the win' whan 'twas blawn;
I seldom was blest wi' a stockin' or shoon,
An' bannet nor cap never happit my croun.
But youngsters, like auld fowks, are nae aye content,
On a new penny whistle my min' it was bent;
I dream'd o't by nicht an' thocht o't by day,
An' the bonny sweet notes I thocht it wad play.
But Marywell market, the last o' its race,
Like the last o' oor years, was comin' apace;
The day cam' at last, an' a blithe ane to me,
I thocht ither fowk like mysel' were in glee.
I scrubbit my face an' gat on a clean sark,
My toilet indeed it was nae mickle mark;
An' tho' tatter't my dress, my face wore a smile,
The road it was short, about half a Scotch mile.
There were whistles an' whittles, an' penguns galore,
An' ginchbread an' sweeties an' toys, great store

Were laid out to please ilka costomer's e'e,
A' wi' the intention to catch a bawbee.
The chapmen were plenty, some roarin' aloud,
" My wares are the best, an' nane half so gude ;
Here whistles a penny, that's weel worth a groat,
I sell them so cheap 'cause I sta' a' the lot."
I soon coft a whistle, and aff thro' the fair,
To see the queer fowk an' things that were there ;
The spoons and the ladles, the caups and the cogs,
The wobs o' grey hodden and gude Forfar brogues.
An' there wi' the lave, was auld Johnnie Lowrie,
Wi' apples, he said, fae the braw Carse o' Gowrie.
An' up on the hillock sat Aberdeen Kate,
Wi' haddies an' spaldins, and rowth o' fresh skate ;
The melee o' tongues, an' the noise an' the habble,
Wad minded a chiel o' the warkmen at Babel.
Some chattin' at Gaelic an' some at braid Scotch,
Some English, some Irish, and some at hotch-potch ;
An' fouth o' Birse bodies, wi' bannets fu' braid,
The rim it was blue an' the nap it was red ;
An' wives wi' short kirtles an' wallies were seen,
Wi' frowdies an' ribbons wad dazzled yer e'en ;
An' bonny young lasses a' busket fu' trim,
Wi' pouches o' fairin' near fu' to the brim.
But the sun soon began to fa' doun i' the west,
An' the dim shades o' nicht were gath'rin' in haste ;
Syne young fowks an' auld fowks were leavin' the fair,
Nae thinkin' again they wad never meet there.
Some gaed awa' hame an' some gaed to the Craft,
An' pree'd Janet's ale until nearly half daft ;
The Blacksmith an' Cobbler, aye better freens grew,
The Weaver said, " Wife, that's fine ale that ye brew."
But puir Will the weaver, he gat a sad fricht,
His wife cam' aboot him wi' gude mornin' licht,
Wi' a rung in her nieve, leish't him aff doun the Clacnan,
While the gossips a'roun' were a' teetin' and lauchin' ;
An' Johnnie the blacksmith, a gude honest bodie,
That day he gaed hame an' he fell owre the studdy ;
But Sandy the souter, his thrapple was gizzen,
He took a' the neist day to weet his dry wizzen ;
An' Jock the piper an' Willie the miller,
Drank wi' the Souter as lang's he had siller.
Sin' that day to this, there are saxty an' some
O' simmers an' winters that's noo gaen an' come,
The Marywell Market stood mony a day,
Tho' how lang it was there nae bodie can say ;
Wi' houses an' yardies, the spat's covered o'er,
Whaur langsyne the pedlars' spread out their braw store.
But ilka thing comes to an en' at the last,
The Marywell Market's a thing o' the past.

FINZEAN PHOTOS

Ploughing on Ennochie c.1928. Hector Smith with Davie Brown (on right), the foreman.

Dubston 1923/4. Gordon Webster, the son of the tenant, before he left to join the police.

Unknown ploughman, possibly on Wester Clune. Circa 1920s. It was a common practise for someone to stand in front of the horses and wave a hankerchief to make them appear more alert for the photo. The older horse is on the landward side.

Out ferreting c.World War 1. Rt.to left: Ewan Macloed (keeper), John Thow (Ennochie), Archibald Robertson (Percie).

———— The Whisky Trail ————

1792. The Rev. Joseph Smith, Minister of Birse, recorded:
"In 1791 one family emigrated to Philadephia...An unmarried woman remained; she regrets that she did not go with the rest, for, says she,'Troubles are only beginning here'. We trust she is not inspired with the gift of prophecy."

1842. The Rev. George Smith, Minister of Birse, recorded:
"... a considerable number of families, formerly supported by illicit distillation, have been obliged to remove to the towns and other parishes: a good many families, also, have emigrated to America".

———————

In the fifty years between these two reports above, the number of illicit stills and the extent of whisky smuggling reached their greatest extent in Birse and then came to an abrupt end. Nowadays whisky is acclaimed as Scotland's national drink and visitors are led around the 'Whisky Trail' as if it were a critical part of our cultural heritage. It is often forgotten that the development of Scotland's modern distilling industry meant the end of the road for many of the population of a parish like Birse.

Before the eighteenth century, whisky distillation for home and local consumption was the tradition in many Scottish communities. Bere (the old form of barley) was still grown as the main cereal in preference to oats and the conversion of the grain into whisky was, apart from anything else, a very effective way of storing this perishable crop. At the beginning of the 1700s, the new British government imposed a Malt Tax; a move that was so unpopular in Scotland that a parliamentary vote in 1713 to split the Union because of it, was only defeated by four votes. This intrusion by government on a traditional activity was resented by the rural population and to continue distilling without paying the tax was not regarded as a crime in most local communities. It did however, mean that much local production became illicit and a whisky smuggling trade had started in Aberdeenshire by the 1720s. At this time though, the extent of whisky consumption in Scotland was very limited. It was only the traditional drink in preference to ales in certain areas and everywhere the landowners, ministers and other gentlemen drank brandy, gin or claret.

The real growth of illicit distilling and whisky smuggling began in the 1780s. This was due to several factors. At the general level, there was an increasing population and expanding urban cash economy which, together with an easing of the alcohol retail licensing system, resulted in more consumption of drink in Scotland as a whole. Also, brandy, gin and claret started to be subject to rising tariffs and interuptions of supply because of the wars with France. The growth of the high class market for whisky is reflected in the statement for Aberdeenshire that 'all ranks since 1785, have become exceedingly partial to whisky'. Whisky had the great advantages of low cost and easy availability and it was on top of this that government regulation had the effect of ensuring this demand was met illicitly. Before 1786 anyone could operate a still of less than twelve gallons capacity for their own use, but in that year still licensing was adapted so that no-one could have a still of less than forty gallons. Further, the license cost 20/- per gallon, or at least £40, and within ten years this had risen to £100. The government's revenue need for the Napoleonic wars also resulted in steady increases in the Malt Tax in the last decades of the eighteenth century and rapid rises in the early nineteenth century. The result of these two changes was, firstly, to make the majority of producers illegal and ,secondly, to cause a reduction of quality in the legal product. The larger, licensed producers started to try and save money by using a high proportion of unmalted, or raw, grain and pushing production through their stills as fast as possible.

By the end of the eighteenth century, the illicit trade of small scale production in and around the Highlands, with organised bands of smugglers leading the whisky across the passes to the lowland market, was fully established. This illicit whisky was much favoured by all because of its superior quality and was selling at a higher price than the legal brew. The trade continued to grow. Between 1799 and 1813 the legal production of whisky often had to stop because of high war grain prices. Then in 1814 the government banned any still under 500 gallons (later modified to 200), so that by 1816 it was estimated that at least half the whisky drunk in Scotland was illicit.

Official attempts to stop the huge illegal trade during this period were very unsuccessful. The local communities had a solidarity over what had been a traditional activity and excise officers, normally local men, were either corrupted or else unable to tackle the strength of the smugglers' caravans. Farmers supported the trade as they could obtain at least twenty percent more than the open market price of bere by selling to the illicit distillers. The landowners, who were also the magistrates, acquiesced to the trade because it allowed them to collect higher rents than would otherwise have been possible from much of their land and because of the illicit bottles on their own tables.

The **main zone** for illicit stills was the Highland fringe around the rich arable growing areas. Birse was a classic location. Each farm was likely to have had its own still. In one corner of the parish for example, each of Powlair, Bogmore, Tillyorn and Wester Clune are known to have had one and at them it was a common practice to put on the boiler and hang out some blankets to disguise the presence of steam from the still. The main practitioners were however, the crofters and cottars. It was an operation which needed little starting capital. The grain would be purchased on credit from the farmer and only repaid as a revenue came in from the final product. The still itself needed to be small to avoid detection, normally a bothie only eight feet square cut into a brae side in some remote corner of the parish, for example in Birse, at the back of Peter Hill, at the base of the Slough Craigs and in the hollow below Craigentoul Hill known as Bogranda. The site had to be carefully selected to avoid any smoke been seen, although the distilling could be carried out in broad daylight by using old stumps of burnt heather and juniper bushes to make a fire without smoke. Apart from access to a stream, the requirements at the bothie were: a portable handmill, the vat, the boiler and the cooler, the still, the head and the worm with the flakestand, and the redder for stirring up the material in the vat. A bothie would be worked by two or three people who pooled their resources for the £2-3 necessary to equip it. Most of the distilling was done in the late autumn/ early winter when the grain was in, the burns full and everybody returned from seasonal labour. The finished whisky was stored for a time in skins or hardwood kegs and then sold to the smugglers who carried it south on a string of ponies, often disguised as loads of peat. The dregs of the still and the draff (spent grain) also had their value; they provided a useful suppliment feed for the cattle at a time of the year when the grazing was lean.

These crofters and cottars who did the illicit distilling, were the poor who had least to lose and most to gain by defying the law. It was not a means of becoming rich for they were squeezed between the farmers, who charged over the market price for the grain, and the professional smugglers, who controlled the final price and often took a mark up of 100% or more to themselves. It was these, the farmers and smugglers, together with the landowners and the higher rents they charged, who made most out of the traffic. For the crofters and cottars the trade provided a vital means to pay the rent and, as Sir G.S.Mckenzie of Coull, a neighbouring parish to Birse, observed, 'they must do it or starve'. The local Justices of the Peace knew, as landowners, that they could not enforce the law properly as it would result in wholesale depopulation. The government's regulations on whisky between 1780 and 1820 had both ensured that much of the market would be supplied illicitly and outlawed a traditional activity at a time when the rural population had to increasingly depend upon it. While the illicit trade succeeded it enabled the old order to survive and so through the first two decades of the nineteenth century the population of Birse and many similar parishes increased.

Two major government investigations in 1821 and 1822 exposed the full extent to which the law was being flouted and the scale of potential revenue being lost. To combat the illegal trade two laws were introduced. The 1822 Illicit Distillation (Scotland)Act increased the fines due, allowed searches without permits from JPs and introduced new penalties for those allowing the practice on their estates. The 1823 Excise Act reduced the duty on a gallon of whisky by over half and also reduced the license fee to a uniform low level. Together these laws had an immediate effect on crushing the illicit trade. The Excise law eroded the cost advantages of illicit production, while at the same time allowing the major conventional distillers to increase their malt content and slow down production, so greatly improving the quality of the licensed product. The 1822 law was successful both because it was combined with closer supervision of the courts to see what the fines were actually imposed and because specialised squads of soldiers and sailors were used to assist the excise officers against the bands of smugglers. There were violent clashes between them for the next decade, but by then the traffic in illicit whisky was virtually extinct. Important changes that assisted this success were that the farmers no longer needed to support the illicit distillers for the grain trade and that a rapidly growing number of landowners were discovering that they could increase their rents by carrying out improvements on their estates, instead of needing to turn a blind eye to illegal practices.

The effect on the number of people able to earn a living in Birse was immediate. After reaching a peak in 1827, the population went into sharp decline. To quote the minister in 1842, "The cause of the advance and subsequent decline was the same, viz. the illict distillationof whisky.While this infamous and demoralising practice prevailed, population increased through the facilities by which families were maintained among the hills and valleys on its profits But no sooner was this system put down, than the effect appeared on the population". The loss of this essential income to the crofters and cottars meant that the 'whisky trail' was no longer a traffic across the mounth passes, but rather a road that led the distillers themselves away from their native parish to the towns and to emigration overseas.

Several stories exist from Birse in the 1820s and '30s of clashes or narrow escapes with the gauger, Malcolm Gillespie, who was a notoriously successful excise officer on Deeside. One concerns the look-a-like brothers John and James Glass, who crofted in the Forest. John, who made his living by poaching and smuggling, was living in the hills because of the heat from Gillespie, and only came home at night for food and occasionally for a few hours sleep. One of these times Gillespie and his men arrived to arrest John, but James managed to change places with him and the triumphant gaugers set off towards Aberdeen with the wrong man. It was only when they were nearing the area of the Bucket Mill that James revealed the mistake to his captures. The infuriated Gillespie remembered stories of the brothers'likeness and, after stopping at two houses to test James' identity, reluctantly released him.

Even when smuggling had been stopped, production continued for local consumption. Such is perhaps implied in the Rev.George Smith's comment on the inhabitants of Birse:"...the chief excesses whereof they are guilty, arising from the abuse of ardent spirits, into which a good many occasionally fall, from the facilities with which spirits are to be had". Certainly stories of encounters with the gaugers continue at least until the beginning of the twentieth century and it is recalled that a sheet used to be hung out at the old post office at Whitehills,in Finzean,to warn of the approach of the gaugers over the hill from Ballater. The last still in the parish, although not an active one, was not removed until the 1900s from Finzean sawmill and now all that is left are the rumours of the locations of still buried casks.

A DETACHED PORTION

The whole of Scotland is divided into parishes. There are about 900 in total; some 90 are in Aberdeenshire of which Birse is the southern-most. The precise origin of Scotland's parishes is not known, but they are quite old. Birse, for example, is first recorded from a charter of the 10th August 1157. The 825th anniversary of this was marked in 1982 by a small exhibition of local history material in Birse Church.

The boundaries of parishes are usually natural features such as a watershed or else some clear man-made march like a prominent road. However, there have been noted exceptions to this and one involved Birse parish. Until the late nineteenth century there was a detached portion of Aboyne and Glen Tanar parish situated in the midst of Birse. This was a small island of 349 acres which was seven miles by road from the main part of its own parish.

In 1890, this detached portion consisted of the two seventy acre farms of Percie and Dalsack, Percie Croft, Woodside of Percie, the South Lodge, a house on the Forest road and fourteen small houses around the sawmill and Percie, together with an area of planted woodland. The population was then 47 persons, but it had once been higher (e.g. 70 in 1819).

It is not clear how Percie and Dalsack came to be a detached portion of Aboyne and Glen Tanar. In most early documents, such as the 1511 rent roll, they are listed as being part of the Bishops of Aberdeen's lands in Birse. However, it is likely that this was just for convenience and that they had become detached before that date. The area is treated separately in a charter dated 1419, for example, when Bishop Gilbert granted to Thomas Donaldson 'all his vill of Parsi, now waste and uninhabited'.

The isolation of Percie and Dalsack from the rest of Aboyne created problems both for its residents and for the administrators of Birse. It was difficult for these inhabitants to receive poor relief because of their remoteness and the Minister of Birse commented in the 1790s how often these people had to be given aid from Birse's funds. It was hoped that the suspension bridge, which was built across the Dee at Aboyne in 1828, would alleviate the problem, but it did not solve the issue of poor relief and all the children continued to attend the school in Finzean at Birse's expense.

In 1889, under the Local Government (Scotland) Act, Boundary Commissioners were empowered to modify parish and county boundaries to remove irregularities, and the case of Percie and Dalsack was one of those which they came to consider. It appeared an obvious and natural decision to add them to Birse, but the local politics were more complicated than at first thought. The difficulty was the responsibility of each parish to levy rates to support its own poor and provide its own parish's education. Neither Birse nor Aboyne objected in principle to the detached portion becoming part of Birse, but each found arguments to claim compensation for their respective gain and loss.

Aboyne parish, represented by Lord Huntly, claimed that as they would lose the assessable annual value of Percie and Dalsack of £154, they should receive the north west corner of Birse close to Aboyne, which had a nearly equivalent value of about £200.

Birse, represented by W.E. Nicol of Ballogie, dismissed this claim as not even a serious contention. Birse argued that firstly no good boundary could be found in the north west corner to replace the present one which was natural and clearly defined. Secondly, the west end of Birse was the most valuable portion of the whole parish, being already feued to a certain extent. It was the only part of Birse from which the parish could hope for increased value.

Instead, Birse Parochial Board adopted the stance that they did not want to accept Percie and Dalsack in the first place as it would be a burden on them. Rather than give anything as compensation they claimed that they should be compensated. Birse's parochial rate was seven pence in the pound and the school rate sixpence in the pound. This would produce a revenue of £8.6.10 from Percie's valuation but when the expense of the aliment for the two paupers registered in Percie, Andrew Smart and Wm. Ross, was deducted this gave a loss of £5.19.2. Moreover, this loss included only aliment and not extras such as coals or clothes that might be required by the paupers. The number of small houses at Percie was also pointed out. Apart from the farms, a croft and a cottar house, only three of the houses had a valuation of £5 or over, there being eleven houses under £4 rental. It was argued that the number of this very undesirable class of house on Percie must be a prolific source of pauperism.

Birse also argued that if any change was to be made to the parish's boundaries, it should be by transferring Balnacraig from Aboyne to Birse. This would make the Dee the obvious and natural boundary to Birse. As it was, Balnacraig was entirely cut off from Aboyne by the river and was five miles away by road.

The addition of Balnacraig to Birse would also have helped cancel out the loss incurred by the parish if Percie and Dalsack were to be added. Balnacraig's value was £510 and this would yield £27.12.6., less £25.0.6. for four paupers, giving a gain of £2.12.0. To support this case, W.E. Nicol, who was also the owner of Balnacraig, presented a letter to the Boundary Commissioners, signed by all the inhabitants of Balnacraig, in which they 'earnestly begged that it should be transferred to Birse because of the inconvenience they suffered by being completely cut off from Aboyne'.

The first meeting by the representatives of Birse and Aboyne with the Commissioners was on the twenty seventh of July 1890. It recommended that delegates from the Parochial and School Boards of each parish should meet to try and resolve their differences. This took place on the 19th August, but failed to resolve the issue. Neither side was prepared to give up the portion which the other side was claiming as compensation.

The Commissioners, meeting in Edinburgh on the 7th October to consider the evidence before them, adopted that Percie and Dalsack should be transferred to Birse with no other changes. The transfer was to take effect from the first of January 1891 for the election of School Boards and from the fifteenth of May 1891 for all other purposes.

FRANK RAMSAY, "BIRSE", JAMAICA

Frank Ramsay was born in the early 1780s, the eldest son of Francis Ramsay, merchant at Haugh of Birsemore. In 1798 he was awarded a Gilbert Ramsay Bursary to study at Aberdeen University. When he graduated in 1802 he left his native parish and went, like many young men from Deeside at that time, to seek his fortune in Jamaica. Frank's employment in Jamaica was already arranged before he set out: he was bound to be an apprentice to Mr. Alexander Garden, Surveyor, at £80 for the first year, £100 for the second and £120 for the third year.

On the 27th November 1802, Frank left Aberdeen by boat for London, arriving after four and a half days. Within only forty-eight hours, he had secured through an agent a passage on the ship 'Merlin' to Jamaica. He paid his fare with ten guineas of his own money and a draft for a further twenty guineas from Mr. Garden. Frank arrived at Morant Bay in East Jamaica on the 11th February 1803, after a nine and a half week voyage during which he was often seasick.

Frank gave up his apprenticeship after two years, which was the period by when one was considered completely seasoned, and moved out of Port Morant to work on the Airy Castle Estate. His wage on the plantation was only £70 per annum, but Frank reckoned he could save more than he had managed out of his apprenticeship wage while living in the town.

Postal charges from Jamaica were high and Frank only wrote home two or three times a year when he had the opportunity to send letters with friends returning to Britain. He was, however, doing a deal with his brother John, in Glasgow, by shipping him rum in exchange for items from home. He also offered his father a puncheon of rum which contained 220-250 Scotch pints of spirit, said to be far stronger than the best whisky made in Birse. But he warned his father against accepting it unless he could be sure of selling it, as the duty would be around £60. There were also other hazards: some clothes that had been sent out to Frank were lost when the ship 'Hunter' was wrecked on the Irish coast near Wicklow.

In the spring of 1805, martial law was declared in Jamaica because of the threat from a large French fleet in the area. All white people were required to do duty with the regular troops, and Frank was surprised to find that the soldier's life was less disagreeable than he had heard it represented. Reinforcements of ships arrived from England at the end of April, but rumours still persisted that the French fleet, with 20,000 troops on board, was on its way to the Island.

The atmosphere caused by the French fleet was bad for business and was made worse by rumours that the British parliament was about to abolish slave trading. Frank reckoned that it would ruin the already miserable living on the Island and felt the people in Britain had it wrong. He argued that the slaves were far better off than the labouring poor in Scotland. They were well fed, clothed and lodged. There was a hospital on each estate where they were visited by a white physician when they were sick. They were allowed to sell goats, hens and hay for extra income and the law explicitly forbade the giving of more than thirty-nine lashes. Furthermore, these were apparently laid on lightly and Frank had only witnessed one or two instances where a negro had received a more severe flogging than he himself had received from his old schoolmaster in Birse, Mr. Cromar.

By 1807, when slave trading was abolished in the British Empire (slavery itself was not outlawed until 1833), Frank was back to surveying. He was now employed by a Mr. Keiffer in Kingston, who had a lot of business in hand. Shortly afterwards his brother John arrived from Scotland. Although John landed only half a mile from where Frank was now living, he went to the old address over fifty miles away and it was four months before they made contact, by which time John was working on an estate as a book-keeper.

In the autumn of 1810 Frank went into partnership with Mr. Keiffer but was immediately laid low by ill health. The fall was invariably an unhealthy time of year, but 1810 seems to have been a particularly bad year with many young men dying, including several of Frank's friends from the North-east. Frank recovered however and during the following year he and Mr. Keiffer still had plenty of work, but payment was hard to procure: Frank seems to have extended credit too far through over-confidence in others. This was a time when there were many bankruptcies and no confidence in any sector of business. The effect of stopping the slave trade was being made worse by the blockade of European ports in 1812-1813, which depressed the price of coffee.

In 1814, Frank bought a property at St. David, which he named "Birse". It was a financial gamble that almost failed to pay off because Frank broke his leg soon after when jumping a stone wall and was laid up for three months. However, "Birse" was to remain his home for the next ten years despite continuing poor business and the fact that Frank's health was now deteriorating.

By 1818, Frank was anticipating coming to Scotland for a visit, but in each successive year either poor health or a lack of money prevented him. He might have made it in 1823, but he bought an additional piece of ground. He had hoped to sell it at a quick profit, but had difficulty in finding a buyer. In 1824 Frank at last managed to book a passage home for his long awaited holiday. After a voyage of eight weeks and two days, he wrote to his mother from London, (his father had died two years before) advising her that she should not expect a rich West Indian, but one who had been compelled to try to restore his lost health by the assistance of his native air.

Frank brought his ten year old son Thomas with him. He was to be left behind in Birse for his education, as this had been rather neglected in Jamaica. Frank himself stayed in Scotland for a year. The last that is known of him is from a letter dated London 23rd October 1825. He was waiting there to find a passage back to Jamaica, now over forty years old and without the optimism of his first voyage.

By 1825, Frank's elder brother Thomas was tenant of Haugh of Birsemore. One of his younger brothers, William (born 1789), was tenant of Waterside. William's descendants have farmed Waterside throughout the 150 years since that time. His eldest son Francis (1819-1897) succeeded him; his son James (1858-1932) followed and then his son James (1899-1964). This last James was succeeded by James Garioch, whose mother was one of James Ramsay's three sisters, the last of whom died in 1980.

The Legend

Old parchments lay before me, old deeds of men long dead,
Who took a deal of pains to write, and thought of what they said;
And among these time-worn papers of the property of Birse
There was one that set me thinking - A quaint old fashioned curse
The manuscript was blotched and old, the writing hard to read
But this is what it meant to say, and that is all we need:
"Whene'er a Laird of Birse shall die, on midnight of that day
Death on a horse shall gallop up and bear his soul away."

Eh, proudly reared the turrets once of that old stately pile,
Where bravery and honesty had dwelt so long awhile,
And scarred and battered parapets bore witness of the ways
Its doors and walls were treated in the old Invaders' days.
Alas! those walls are crumbling; alas those doors are gone;
Its glory and its valour and its people all are done:
The nettle grows and flourishes where stood the festive board,
And owls and bats infest the halls where once dwelt Birse's lord.

There comes a sound of revelry, though near the hour of morn,
For forty years ago that day The Laird of Birse was born,
And all his friends for miles around to-day are gathered there,
To do honour to the house of Birse and justice to its fare.
There are chieftains from the banks of Don, and from the braes of Dee
Hard men to meet in angry moods, but goodly men to see.
Forbes had proposed his "Country" and Esslemont "The King",
And Johnnie Coutts of Castletown had just been asked to sing,
When from the table's farther end there rose a mighty cheer,
For Huntly had arisen, Scotland's first and proudest peer.
"For twice two hundred years", he cried "our lands have marched with Birse".
His folk and mine together fought for better and for worse,
And I am proud to rise to-night, once before you all,
And wish my neighbour happiness in his ancestral hall.
The history of our fathers has a glorious lesson taught,
For liberty and honour have they been boldly fought,
Look through the deeds of Scotland, at the souls forever fled,
And find a man of all our clan of whom 'twas ever said,
"He betrayed his King and country to further some design."
Then may my God curse every clod belonging me and mine;
And may we in the future, in the days that are to be,
When the years have dragged us downward, as the waters of the Dee
Cast the pine-stems from Glentanar in the ocean's breast at last
May we look back with pleasure on a bright and peaceful past;
May we glide down Life's river with this great aim in view -
to do unto our neighbours as we should wish them to do"

# of Birse

Loud was clink of glasses, and hearty the applause
And then a silence seemed to fall for no apparent cause;
Maybe they just awaited for their worthy host to rise
But reasons for such lulls as these no person can surmise.
Whilst still the silence lasted, there broke on every ear
The well-known sound - on the distant ground, a horseman drawing near.
Clattering, clattering, clattering, nearer and nearer it grew,
And the strong and the hale turned stern and pale, for each the story knew.
Galloping, frenziedly galloping - each man put his hand to his dirk -
The rider drew near the castle door, and stopped with a sudden jerk.
They heard the clank of heavy spurs as he mounted the granite stairs;
Of the squires and the lords, some drew their swords, and some merely muttered
                                                                prayers.
He paused at the door for a moment, then loudly rang the bell,
And each seemed to feel it was no one real, but a messenger from Hell;
Or why did not someone answer the door? Why did they not go to see.
But tho' each man heard, not a servant stirred to learn who this might be
Then up rose Grant of Dinnet; fiercely hissed he, "By the powers
No honest folk can brook a joke at these unseemly hours.
Now I, with your permission, will answer to this bell,
And short and sharp must the story be this horseman has to tell,
Yes, by the gods above me, and by my father's name,
'Twill be quickly said, or I'll strike him dead, and his, not mine, the blame."
With this he drew his claymore and passed into the hall,
And many rose and followed him - Birse never moved at all,
He lay quite helpless in his chair, with face so set and pale.
Was it only fear that his hour was near, or did he believe the tale?
Now came the creak of a bolt shot back, and the fall of a heavy bar.
And a voice cried out, as the door flew back, "Now tell me who you are,"
Only the hoot of an owl near to, only the wind in the trees,
Only a sigh from the brook hard by, only an icy breeze.
But the breeze passed on thro' the outer hall into the banquet room;
It was the breath, they said, of Death, drawing a soul to its doom.
Slowly the guests returned to the hall, gently they bade good-night,
Yet not a word from the Laird was heard, and his hands were cold and white.
They bore him away from the banquet room, his kinsfolk by his side,
But ere the dawn of the coming morn the Laird of Birse had died.
Never the prattle of children now, never a merry shout;
Weird are the calls in the old grey walls, when the light of day goes out;
The herdsmen say that oftentimes, when night enshrouds the moor
They hear a horse spring up the course towards the castle door;
There sounds the clanging of a bell, they see a flickering light,
And then two horsemen gallop up - far out into the night.

FINZEAN PHOTOS

Three generations of Piries at Maryfield Cottage. c.World War 1.

Robert and Joseph Farquharson with tenants, c.World War 1.

OWNER OCCUPATION 1880-1980

The landownership of Birse has stayed very constant since 1870 with the thirty-one and a half thousand acres of the parish being divided between the four estates of Birse, Finzean, Ballogie and Balfour. The only change, apart from some land feued to the Forestry Commission, has been the sale of the 470 acre farm, the Shannel, by Finzean estate in the 1970s.

In 1870, it was only the lairds who owned their own houses. Everybody else was a tenant of one of the estates, apart from the four church ministers. They were listed as the proprietors, by virtue of their office, of the manses owned by their respective churches.

Since 1880, however, the number of people in the parish who own their own houses has grown continuously. Now over 40% of the houses are owned by their occupiers. It is a percentage which is still rapidly increasing, though all these houses have very little land associated with them; usually about a quarter of an acre, but up to three acres in a couple of instances.

This growth has not been because of any overall increase in the number of houses in the parish. Despite the fact that the population has fallen by half in the last hundred years the number of houses has been very steady: 238 in 1880, 227 in 1980. In 1840 there were 284 houses in the parish, although eighteen of these were uninhabited, just as there have usually been at least a dozen vacant houses in the parish at any time right up to the present. In 1791 there were 273 inhabited houses in Birse, while a hundred years earlier still, in 1694, when the population was similar to what it is now, an indication of the number of houses is given by the tax return which recorded 202 hearths in Birse.

While the number of houses has stayed fairly constant over the last one hundred years, there has always been a changing quota of houses. Some have been knocked down, allowed to decay or abandoned to become sheds, while others have been renovated and other new ones built. The total numbers of houses shown for each date in Table 1 are slightly inconsistent because the figures are drawn from the Valuation Rolls. These will often vary to some small degree as to whether uninhabited or uninhabitable houses were listed. Sometimes they might also record each cottage and bothie on a farm separately, while grouping them together at other times.

The figures in Table 1 only include dwelling houses. They exclude schools, shops, halls and other premises like smiddies and sawmills. These later were often 'tenant erections' and were listed with the tenants as proprietors, although they were still on land owned by one of the estates. Some houses were also built by the tenants themselves and are similarly listed. This was necessary because of the Registration of Leases (Scotland) Act 1857, which required the occupiers of properties on leases greater than twenty one years to be described as the proprietors in the Valuation Rolls. The practice of long leasing used to be favoured by many landowners as an alternative to feuing land, particularly for building purposes, or if an 'entail' made an obstacle to feuing land on a particular estate.

Table 1. Number of dwelling houses in Birse by ownership

Year	Finzean	Ballogie	Balfour	Birse	Owner-occupied	Total	% owner occupied
1880	110	60	12	50	6	238	2.5
1890	117	60	12	50	12	252	4.8
1900	105	60	12	48	17	242	7.0
1910	107	56	12	37	19	231	8.2
1920	106	56	12	33	20	227	8.8
1930	106	53	12	34	25	230	10.9
1940	97	51	12	32	25	217	11.5
1950	91	51	13	29	29	213	13.6
1960	97	55	13	29	37	231	16.0
1970	89	55	10	22	48	224	21.4
1980	67	47	7	22	84	227	37.0

Fig.1   The Growth of
Owner-occupation in
Birse,   1880-1980.

Key:

the total number
of owner-occupied houses
in the parish at that time

the number of
owner-occupied houses
added during the previous
decade.

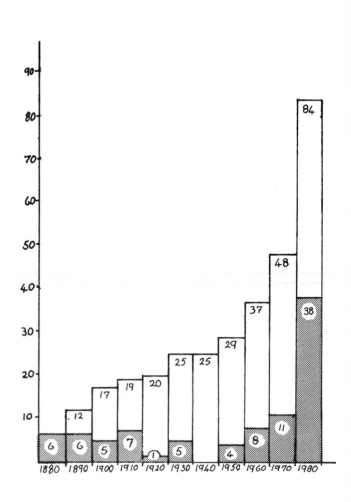

86

In 1880, of the seven properties described in the Valuation Roll as owner occupied, only Craigmore and Aultdinnie were actually feued. The others were on long leases, four of them subsequently becoming actually owner occupied. The one which reverted to Birse estate was Goodwood Cottage. In 1880 Alex. Begg, labourer, was listed as proprietor, in 1890 he was still there, though describing himself as a fencer. In 1900 Henry Kelly, colporteur, was there but as a straightforward tenant.

Between 1880 and the First World War, the growth of owner occupation was entirely in the north-west corner of the parish next to Aboyne. The five tenant proprietors amongst the first nineteen owners can be identified by their occupations: shoemaker, river-watcher, widow, gamekeeper and gardener. Of the other fourteen, half reflect the nature of the new housing development: three architects, a stone merchant and three builder/masons. The other seven were all wealthy: two Colonels, one Major, a Clothier from Albyn Place in Aberdeen, the Town Clerk of Aberdeen and a Wood Merchant with a sawmill at Cults.

The first developments in owner occupation occured on Birse estate when it was owned by the Marquis of Huntly and continued when he sold out to the American Robert Heaven in 1897, but ceased when he in turn sold the estate to the Cowdrays in 1912. Between the two World Wars there was little further development of owner occupation in the parish. A number of small 'tenant-properties' surfaced in Finzean and the first dwelling on the Shooting Greens appeared in the Valuation Rolls. The local authority also became the proprietor of some dwelling houses when it built six cottages at Woodside, Birse, in the 1930s, and to which Praesmor was added as an Eventide Home by 1950.

The rate of increase of owner occupation has been becoming steadily faster since 1940. A dozen properties were added in the twenty years up to 1960, while the same number were added in the next ten years to 1970. Then, during the 1970s, more owner occupied properties were created than during all the preceding decades of this century. The distribution of these properties was, up to 1960, half within Birse estate, a couple in Finzean, a couple on the Shooting Greens, and two were redundant manses. In the period 1960-70, half were again within Birse estate and half in Finzean. Then during the ten years until 1980, more than half were in Finzean, with the remainder being on Birse estate, or else for the first time on Balfour and Ballogie estates.

By 1980 eighty four, or 37%, of the dwelling houses in Birse were owner occupied and the figure has already passed 40% in the last two years due to further sales by Finzean estate. It is a trend of increasing owner occupation in Birse which might be anticipated by its location. The first developments took place near Aboyne in the late Victorian/Edwardian era when it was fashionable to retire to a villa on Deeside, and then the surge during the last ten to fifteen years as the parish became within commuting distance of Aberdeen. However, the distribution of owner occupation does not necessarily match this overall pattern so much as the particular policies of the individual estates.

The initial selling on Birse estate appears to have resulted from the financial difficulties of both the Marquis of Huntly and Robert Heaven. The sales on that estate during the last thirty years have been due to two other factors. The first has been Birse estate's position as a peripheral unit in the Cowdrays extensive landholdings. On both Birse and their other peripheral holdings, dwellings have been sold as part of a rationalisation of surplus assets. The other factor has been the small, but significant multiplication of houses within the owner occupied sector (e.g. the servants cottage to one of the Victorian mansions being sold to become a separate property).

On Balfour estate the creation of owner occupied properties in the last ten years occured at the hand over of generations, cottages being sold when the sons of the late laird took over. Just as the sales on Birse estate have been a typical outcome for a peripheral estate, so the reduction of tenanted property on Balfour has matched the trend on most very small estates. Finzean and Ballogie estates, on the other hand, show what very different approaches can be adopted on two similar sized estates lying adjacent to each other.

Finzean estate, which has been selling tenant properties whenever they have become vacant, as well as occasional building plots, has recently extended this to include selling to the sitting tenants in several instances. In comparison, Ballogie has sold virtually no properties, those that become empty being allowed to remain so. In Finzean's case it is part of a wider strategy of reducing the estate's commitments and making capital available for landuse developments within the estate. In Ballogie poor water supply has been responsible for the lapse of some properties, but with most it appears to have been the estate's lack of will or need to sell, combined with the uneconomic return of doing up the houses themselves and renting them out.

The positions of all four estates reflect the approaches of many estates in Scotland, however, Birse also has one group of houses that occupy a very unusual position relative to Scottish landownership. This is the colony on the Shooting Greens. The Shooting Greens survived as a relic Crown Common, over which the neighbouring estates had rights, until as recently as 1960, when it passed to the Forestry Commission. There have been people living on the Shooting Greens throughout the period considered here (1880-1980). Initially, though, it was just seasonally in the self built turf houses. Some of Deeside's flock masters used to pass parts of the winter there with a few hundred ewes and woodcutters, working in the Blackhall forest, lived there for the duration of their contracts. In the early years of this century, there were people like Willie Riddler and Jimmy Clark, who used to sell baskets and bissoms around the neighbourhood, staying there.

Since the 1930s, there has been a tendency for the various bothies on the Shooting Greens to become permanent houses recorded in the Valuation Rolls. What is now known as Captain Hamilton's house was a bothie started by a woodcutter, Bisset, while Whinbrae used to be a shed, where William Fraser of Adendale Croft, Strachan, kept hens and made wooden barrows. Two of the other houses were also wood-cutters bothies, built by David Stewart, father of George Stewart at Cults farm. The other property, Langakumen, was built by Alexander Freeland, a member of the well-known Aberdeenshire fishing family. The name of his property derives from the length of time it took when he tried to obtain title deeds for his cottage off the Crown Commissioners.

The Shooting Greens is an exceptional episode which is unlikely to develop much further. The increase in owner occupation in the rest of the parish, however, looks set to continue. The way that it is happening, the sale of landless houses at high market prices, tends to make it part of a trend that goes much further back than the beginnings of owner occupation in 1880. The trend is the dissociation of the population in Birse from the land there.

In the hundred years before 1880, the changes in housing were part of the replacement of the old collective fermtouns by larger single tenanted farm and marginal crofts. Many people in the parish lost their direct involvement with the land, often ending up as landless farm workers. Now the crofts have been absorbed and the farms are either amalgamated or taken in hand by the estates. The houses, like the cottages left by the declining number of estate employees and farm workers, become empty and are sold. The new buyers are typically either buying a house for their retirement, or else, as a place to live in the countryside while they commute to work, usually in Aberdeen. After the changes in the nineteenth century, which broke the link with the land for many, the trend now is for an increasing number of the people to not even have any connection at all with the parish. Birse is becoming suburban.

With Wolfe at Quebec

In September 1756, after the outbreak of the Seven Years War, fifteen British foot regiments were ordered to raise second battalions. The 32nd was one of several English regiments ordered to find recruits in Scotland and the county of Aberdeen was part of the area assigned to it.

Aberdeenshire was to find 165 men, based on its share of the national Land Tax assessment. The impressed men were to be between the ages of 17 and 45, free of ruptures, above 5 feet 4 inches in height and unemployed. The recruitment was organised by a county committee of Justices of the Peace and Commissioners of Supply, which in turn set up local committees of landowners covering twenty districts. Birse was grouped with Kincardine O'Neil, Lumphanan and Leochel and together they had to produce six men, two of them from Birse.

Local constables were appointed to select the men and many abuses were recorded in the methods they used to impress men and secure the 20/- bounty for each one. The situation was also complicated by two Highland regiments recruiting in the same area, namely Fraser's and Montgomeries Highlanders.

Once the first recruitment was over, it was decided that another 108 men needed to be raised from Aberdeenshire, with only one being required from Birse. Adam Birse, who was named in Birse managed to escape the constables in March 1758 and so evade enlistment, but John Birse was impressed. These men were probably both relatives of William Birse of Calurg, who had fought for the Jacobites at the Battle of Falkirk a dozen years before.

The fate of the recruits from Birse is not known. However, when their regiments reached North America to fight the French, there was one professional soldier there from Birse: David Ochterlonie of Tillyfruskie. His grandfather, James Ochterlonie, and father, David O. Ochterlonie, had both been lairds there. David himself went to Aberdeen University 1743-47. He then served with distinction as a Lieutenant in the Scots Dutch Brigade and was admitted into the Royal American Regiment at the same rank at the beginning of the Seven Years War.

At the seige of Louisbourg, Ochterlonie's gallantry and his military skills were noted by General Amherst and he was promoted to Captain in command of a company in Monckton's regiment (the second battalion, 60th Foot).

On 31st July 1759, David Ochterlonie took part in an attack on Quebec. The previous night he had been wounded in a duel with a brother officer, Captain Wetterstrom, a German serving with the Grenadiers. However, despite this, Ochterlonie still took his place in the landing craft that were being used for the advance. Once ashore, the British troops were soon in trouble from the French sharp-shooters up above them on the Plains of Abraham. When the attack was abandoned Ochterlonie was left lying seriously wounded half a mile from the waiting boats. Beside him on the battlefield was Ensign Henry Peyton with a shattered knee-cap.

As the withdrawal proceeded the Indian allies of the French started coming amongst the wounded in search of scalps. Two approached Ochterlonie, but the Ensign shot the first with his musket and got the other with his bayonet as the Indian came at him. Next to pass by was a straggler from Fraser's Highlanders, who offered the Captain his help. David Ochterlonie replied "Friend, I thank you, but with respect to me, the musket or scalping knife will only be a more speedy deliverance from pain. I have but a few minutes to live. Go, make haste and tender your service where there is a possibility that it may be useful".

By the time the Ensign and Highlander had reached the boats both had received further wounds and Ochterlonie was in danger again. This time it was a French grenadier who saved him from another Indian's knife, although not before he had been stabbed in the stomach. He was then carried to safety by French Officers. When General Wolfe heard of this he despatched a French prisoner to Montcalm, the French general, with a £20 reward. However, the money was returned with the message that an act of mercy needed no reward.

Three days later, Ochterlonie died of his wounds in the General Hospital, Quebec, one of the 434 men who lost their lives in the abortive landing. It was not until the 18th September that Quebec fell; Wolfe paying the price of his daring with his own life.

John Robbie's Wife

John Robbie lived at Marywell in Birse towards the end of the sixteenth century. He was married with two daughters, Beatrix and Isobell. His wife was Margaret Ogg, who had a son by a previous marriage to a man called Farquhar.

It was the time when a wave of witch persecution came to Aberdeenshire. In 1563 the Scottish Parliament had decreed death for anyone practising witchcraft or consulting a witch and within a hundred years around four thousand people were executed for this crime. The first great epidemic of killings, and the only one to really affect the north-east, broke out in the 1590s, touched off by the nationwide publicity of the trial of a coven of witches in North Berwick, whose various members confessed after torture to having attempted to bring about the King's death.

In 1597 a coven of witches was uncovered at Lumphanan. A woman, Margaret Bean, named eight other women who had danced with her round a great stone on Craig-leauch hill the Halloween before. This was the traditional time for conferring with the Devil and three of the women Margaret Bean named, before she herself was burnt to death, were Margaret Ogg and her two daughters. Margaret Ogg and Beatrix were brought to trial by the evidence of Robert Ross, William Ross (the farmer of Bogloch), John Ross (the Minister of Lumphanan) and John Duguid, who was one of the judges as well as an accuser.

William Ross could recall several instances where Margaret Ogg had shown herself for a witch. About six years before she had taken her own 'heidleas' (head scarf) and cut it into nine pieces, which was the Devil's number. She had secretly laid these under his byre door and within the same year some ten or twelve of his cattle had died. He also recalled that, at about the same time, she had come to the Burn of Bogloch early one morning and cast water over her head. She had then taken a blanket and by her magic drawn off all the dew on his green to her own house. Then, in January 1597, when William's wife had gone to borrow some green yarn at the house where Margaret was staying with her daughter, Margaret had refused her and had instead blown off a green 'clew' (bundle of yarn) in the wife's face, "wherein she contracted a deidlie disease".

This illness, in which the victim spent half the day burning as if in a fiery furnace, the other half consuming away in a cold sweat, was a special point of witchcraft. Archibald Schivas had also suffered it by Margaret Ogg's hand. He was a burgess in Aberdeen and had caused some of Margaret's possessions to be confiscated because of an unpaid debt. She had cursed him, telling him he would regret it, and soon afterwards he became ill for a long time with the witches sickness. It was also recalled, by John Duguid, that Agnes Ross, the Lady of Auchinhove, who had died of such a disease, had blamed it from her deathbed on Margaret and Beatrix. Twelve years before Agnes Ross had bought a shoulder of mutton off John Duguid at the Mill of Auchinhove and taken it to the house where Margaret was staying with her daughter. Agnes Ross had stayed there all night and then, when she ate some of the meat that Margaret and Beatrix had roasted, she had instantly contracted the illness and continued with it for three-quarters of a year until she died. The Minister, whose duty it was to locate and denounce witches, added that a year before, when a cow held by her son was being served by the bull, Margaret had passed a knife back and forth across it three times to her daughter.

On the fourth of April, 1597, the court found Margaret Ogg guilty on six points of witchcraft and she was ordered to be taken out and bound to a stake, strangled until dead and then burnt to ashes. The case against Beatrix Ogg was not so clear cut, though it was found she was "ane suspicious persone... and that scho is nocht of ane guide lyf" because she kept company with her mother. It was decided that she would be banished from Aberdeenshire for life. This was a much cheaper verdict than execution which, judging from the amounts of money in the surviving accounts for barrels of tar, lengths of tow, bags of kindling and to pay the executioner, seems to have been a very expensive business.

Birse Tea

Tea first started to be drunk in Birse around the middle of the eighteenth century. To begin with it was only "used at breakfast by the higher classes in the parish" (Dinnie p.12); while everybody else still drank milk or home-brewed ale. By 1791 however, the Minister could note that "It must be confessed that what were articles of luxury in our hardy forefathers day, are now become articles that are reckoned necessities, as tea".

Today, tea is found in every house. It is usually one of the first items of hospitality offered to any visitor and it is also normally used for the fly-cup at work breaks. Coffee might be considered its only competitor, but coffee is not so universally enjoyed and is now about twice as expensive as tea.

There is one local variation of tea which is still occasionally served in the parish. This is "Birse Tea", a cup of tea served with a dram of whisky in it. Sugar and milk are added whether these are normally taken or not. "Birse Tea" makes a very pleasant and reviving drink, even for someone who does not like whisky. Apparently its most frequent use was in the days when the post round was done on foot. It was offered to the postie to help him on his way through the winter snow!

The origins of the name "Birse Tea" have been assumed to be linked with this parish. However, in William Alexander's classic of North-east life, 'Johnny Gibb of Gushetneuk' (1871), one of the leading characters serves this recipe of tea and her name is Mrs. Birse. I would be interested to hear from anyone who has come across this term outside Birse or who has any ideas about its origins.

Handknitting

In the fifteenth and sixteenth centuries, when the lands of Birse were owned by the Bishops of Aberdeen, the subsistence agriculture yielded little by way of a cash crop. An important exception was wool and a record survives showing how Bishop Elphinstone used wool from his Birse estate to buy quarrying equipment from Holland.

By the seventeenth century, the home production of wool into handknitted stockings or webs of coarse twilled cloth, had become a useful source of outside income for the people in Birse. The 1696 Poll Book records five weavers in Birse but, over and above that, most women were knitting 'at such times as their other country work permits', and even some of the farmers themselves manufactured lengths of cloth for sale.

At that time, and throughout most of the eighteenth century, nearly all the farmers, crofters and cottars had enough sheep to provide clothing for themselves and their families as well as a good ewe or wedder for the table as required. However, by the middle of the century, as the farming changed from subsistence agriculture with services in kind to an economic system with cash rents, the income from the outside sale of woollen goods had become an essential contribution towards the rent. The stockings, and sometimes mitts, were sent to Aberdeen and sold for export to the Dutch, while the plaiden webs were sold at local fairs and towns. All the women were experts at spinning, carding and dyeing and they could earn more money by knitting than from any kind of work.

During the second half of the century, real white wool could hardly be found because the small traditional breed of sheep had been replaced by the Black Face, whose wool was neither so white nor so fine. As a consequence, while the wool of the six and a half thousand sheep in the parish was being exported, the women had to buy in wool for their knitting. It was at this time that Aberdeen manufacturers opened up three stations in the parish where wool was given out and stockings were taken in monthly. It was said to the hosiers credit that they kept their day punctually whatever the weather.

By the end of the eighteenth century the women could earn about 1/8 - 2/- a week from their knitting if they found their own wool, and slightly less if they worked through the stations. Either way the return they made was smaller than fifty years before. Coarse cloth was still made and in addition, spinning lint-yarn had become a useful source of income. Some flax had been cultivated in the parish since the middle of the century, but only a little as there was no lint mill for miles around. In 1791, however, when the Earl of Aboyne built one at Coull, it provided the necessary incentive and several lint stations were opened in the parish to supply the local women with their raw material. A woman could earn at least as much from spinning as by knitting; she might earn 4d or 5d a day at her wheel, giving 2/- to 2/6 a week.

At this time there were still six handloom weavers in the parish, four of them with apprentices but, although they were earning $2\frac{1}{2}$d to 3d an ell (38.4 inches) compared with 1d thirty years before, inflation meant that their real income was declining. Weaving by these professionals and other members of the community, together with the spinning and knitting and the distillation and export of whisky, were the mainstays of the parish economy. They provided the essential cash to allow the rents to be paid. However, they were all soon to be swept away, overtaken by outside changes. The consequences for the numbers of people that the parish could support were dramatic: the population fell rapidly after the 1820s.

The first trade to go was the lint spinning. It was superseded by the industrial manufacture of cotton and, by 1818, hardly any flax was being grown in the North east. Then, with the 1822 Illicit Distilling (Scotland) Act and 1823 Excise Act, the local production and sale of whisky became illegal. In the 1830s the hand weavers were also deprived of their livelihood by new industrial processes, their bitter demise being felt more in other places apart from Birse. By the 1840s it was only stocking knitting that was left. However, the margin of profit from this the oldest of the money earning rural handicrafts was small and becoming smaller. The wool stations had closed and almost any other kind of work offered a better return. By 1850 it was entirely dead as a business. The Minister of Birse, George Smith, writing in 1842, just before the end of the long tradition of stocking knitting, shows how it lingered as a universal occupation right until the last moment...

"Manufactures - The only manufacture which may be said to exist in the parish, is that of coarse woollen stockings by females. In this manufacture, a good part of the wool clipped from the fleecy inhabitants is consumed. It is customary for those so employed to purchase the annual stock of wool likely to be required by them during the summer season, which, having been carded by the mills in the neighbourhood, is then spun into worsted, and knitted into stockings chiefly during winter. Though the profits in this manufacture be extremely small, yet it affords occupation to a great many females who would otherwise be idle, and furnishes a ready employment for fragments of time. A very expert female will spin and knit a pair of stockings in two days. For these she receives generally from 1s. to 1s.3d. when brought to market; of which sum, however, not more than one-half is the remuneration for her labour, the other half being the price of wool, carding, and spinning. One individual will manufacture about three stones and a half of wool in a year, out of which she will produce from 120 to 130 pairs of stockings. Few of the females so employed are entirely dependent on this work for their subsistence, the profits of it being scarcely sufficient for this purpose. Many of them are partly employed in out-door labour, where they can earn higher wages. In times, however, when such is not to be had, or when the season does not admit of it, or when age and infirmities have debarred them from it, the stockings are the never-failing resource. And so much is this the habitual employment of the females, especially of the elderly and unmarried, that, if a person were to go into the dwelling of such and find the "shank" absent from her hands, he might regard it as an unfailing symptom of indisposition."

The Last Inhabitants Local to the Forest

In the 1750s, thirty years after it was first settled, there were a dozen families living in the Forest of Birse. Half of these were Grants and Cattanachs, the
rest having five other surnames between them. During the next thirty years the
number of families increased so that by the 1780s there were 33 families in the
Forest. A quarter of these were Grants and Cattanachs and the list of other surnames had risen to seventeen. If maiden names are included, the complete total of
names in the Forest was 30.

The last people to have lived all their working lives in the Forest, and to be
descended from one of these initial families, were Henry and Jean Duncan. They
retired from Auchabrack in the early 1970s. James Fenton had moved to the Forest
two hundred years before.

James Fenton and his wife Jean Jack were both born in the 1740s and by the 1770s
had started a family and were farming the Castle holding in the Forest. They had
five children before 1789 when a register of Births and Marriages was started in
the parish. Nothing is known of their first three children, James, Susanna and
Ann. The fourth, William, married Margaret Ross of Ballogie in 1807 and had nine
children in the Forest by 1824. The next son, John, married Helen Grant of Drum-
eachie in 1812 and had three children by 1819, when he was still farming in the
Forest. Nothing is known of two other of James Fenton's children, Elizabeth

Elizabeth Duncan (1870-1950)
at the door of Auchabrack.

(born 1789) and Peter (born 1795). However, in between these two, another son was born from whom the Duncans are descended.

Joseph Fenton (1791-1879) married Margaret Anderson (1796-1874) in 1816. Margaret had also been born in the Forest. They had nine children, the youngest of whom was Elizabeth Fenton (1840-1919). She married David Kerr (1821-1880), the keeper at Burnfoot in the Forest, whose father had been David Kerr of Tuskie Croft in Glencat. They had three children; a son who died aged 12, and two daughters.

One daughter married an Innes and moved to Ballogie. They had a son and a daughter, neither of whom married. Margaret Innes, now in her seventies and living at Mains of Potarch, is the only surviving member of this line.

The Kerrs' other daughter was Elizabeth (1870-1950). She moved from Burnfoot to Ballogie Gates in 1895 to marry George Duncan (1857-1938). After six years she was back in the Forest as, in 1901, George took over the tenancy of Auchabrack. He had been brought up at Holmes, Woodend, Finzean, and was a brother of Alexander Duncan of Finzean Sawmill. Their father is thought to have come to Finzean from the Huntly area.

Before George and Elizabeth Duncan moved to Auchabrack, they had three children in Ballogie. George (1896-1960), who became a wood merchant at Potarch, David (1899-1957), who moved from Auchabrack to Woodend in the 1940s, and Jean, who was six weeks old when she moved to the Forest. A third son, Henry (1907-1977), was born at Auchabrack. None of these four children had children of their own and Jean Duncan, at Laurel Cottage, Finzean, is the last surviving descendent of one of those families to have spent her own life in the Forest.

Henry Duncan (1907-77) seated between the Forest's keeper and the shooting tenant's chauffeur.

Sources

Detached Portion

Birse Parochial Board Minute Book. (AC6/7/1) Regional Archives

Frank Ramsay

Transcript by JimCheyne of Aboyne of letters held by James Garioch.

Handknitting

New and Old Statistical Accounts, 1793 and 1843
Wm.Alexander 'Northern Rural Life' reprint 1981
Ian Carter 'Farm Life in Northeast Scotland 1840-1914'. Donald 1979
Robert Dinnie 'An Account of the Parish of Birse' Aberdeen 1865

John Gordon of Glencat

Memoirs of John Gordon of Glencat' London 1734.
Deeside Field 1931

John Robbie's Wife

Miscellany of the Spalding Club Vol.1 Aberdeen 1841.
C.Smout 'History of the Scottish People' Collins 1969.

King Dardanus

Translation of Boece's Hostoriá Gentis Scotorum by John Bellenden
                                        (Ballantyne) 1833
Fenton Wyness 'Royal Valley' Aberdeen 1968.

Landownership 1800-1980

Statistical Accounts, Dinnie and Fenton Wyness ...op.cit
Kirk Session Minutes. Ch2.595.5. in Scottish Record Office.

Legend of Birse

by Lord Granville Gordon, brother of 11th Marquis of Huntly.
Written Xmas.1893 and published by Bliss, Sands et al. London 1894

Market at Marywell

Robert Dinnie 'Songs and Poems' Privately printed Aberdeen 1876
                        (in McBean Rm. Collection at University)

Meikle Drouth

Birse Church Records   op.cit.

Mortification of Gilbert Ramsay

Records of Marischal College 1593-1860. New Spalding Club 1889
Ramsay Mortification Minutes in Birse Church Records op.cit.

Nicols of Ballogie

Genealogy of the Nicol Family (Kincardine Branch) by W.E.Nicol
                                    privately printed London 1909

Owner occupation

Valuation Rolls for the County of Aberdeenshire.

With Wolfe at Quebec

Fenton Wyness 'Spots from the Leopard' Aberdeen 1971.
Jim Cheyne 'With Broadsword and Dirk' unpub. ms.
Jim Cheyne 'Reluctant Heroes' Northern Scot 1981.

Whisky Trail

Old and New Statistical Accounts, 1793 & 1842, op.cit.
T.M.Devine 'The rise and fall of illicit whisky-making in northern
                Scotland' Scottish History Review, 54, 1975.
Rev.J.Stirton 'Crathie and Braemar' Aberdeen 1925.
Rev.A.L.Kemp 'A Deeside Kirk' Aberdeen 1933.
WRI, Finzean 'A History of Finzean' Local 1967.